W9-DBH-209

8 11

Donated by the
Kiwanis Club of Carrollton
"Golden K"
through Friends of the Library
Matching Funds Program 2002

DISCARD

WEST GA REG LIB SYS
Neva Lomason
Memorial Library

DENZEL WASHINGTON

DENZEL WASHINGTON

Anne E. Hill

CHELSEA HOUSE PUBLISHERS
Philadelphia

Chelsea House Publishers

Editor in Chief	Stephen Reginald
Production Manager	Pamela Loos
Picture Editor	Judy L. Hasday
Art Director	Sara Davis
Managing Editor	James D. Gallagher
Senior Production Editor	Lisa Chippendale

Staff for DENZEL WASHINGTON

Project Editor	Therese De Angelis
Associate Editor	Kristine Brennan
Associate Art Director	Takeshi Takahashi
Designer	Keith Trego
Picture Researcher	Patricia Burns
Cover Illustration	Cliff Spohn

© 1999, 2000, 2001 by Chelsea House Publishers, a subsidiary of
Haights Cross Communications. All rights reserved. Printed and
bound in the United States of America.

The Chelsea House World Wide Web address is
http://www.chelseahouse.com

3 5 7 9 8 6 4

Hill, Anne E., 1974-
    Denzel Washington / by Anne E. Hill.
        96 pp.   cm. — (Black Americans of achievement)
    Includes bibliographical references and index.
    Summary: A biography of the African American actor who rose to
the top of his profession, won an Academy Award, and was named
one of the most popular movie stars in 1998.
    ISBN 0-7910-4692-3
        0-7910-4693-1 (pbk.)
    1. Washington, Denzel, 1954-   —Juvenile literature. 2. Actors—
United States—Biography—Juvenile literature. 3. Afro-American
actors—Biography—Juvenile literature. [1. Washington, Denzel,
1954-   . 2. Actors and actresses. 3. Afro-Americans—Biography.]
I. Title. II. Series.
PN2287.W452H56 1998
791.43'028'092—dc21
    [B]   98-15401
                                                   CIP
                                                    AC

CONTENTS

BLACK AMERICANS OF ACHIEVEMENT

HENRY AARON
baseball great

KAREEM ABDUL-JABBAR
basketball great

MUHAMMAD ALI
heavyweight champion

RICHARD ALLEN
religious leader and social activist

MAYA ANGELOU
author

LOUIS ARMSTRONG
musician

ARTHUR ASHE
tennis great

JOSEPHINE BAKER
entertainer

JAMES BALDWIN
author

TYRA BANKS
model

BENJAMIN BANNEKER
scientist and mathematician

COUNT BASIE
bandleader and composer

ANGELA BASSETT
actress

ROMARE BEARDEN
artist

HALLE BERRY
actress

MARY MCLEOD BETHUNE
educator

GEORGE WASHINGTON
CARVER
botanist

JOHNNIE COCHRAN
lawyer

SEAN "PUFFY" COMBS
music producer

BILL COSBY
entertainer

MILES DAVIS
musician

FREDERICK DOUGLASS
abolitionist editor

CHARLES DREW
physician

W. E. B. DU BOIS
scholar and activist

PAUL LAURENCE DUNBAR
poet

DUKE ELLINGTON
bandleader and composer

RALPH ELLISON
author

JULIUS ERVING
basketball great

LOUIS FARRAKHAN
political activist

ELLA FITZGERALD
singer

ARETHA FRANKLIN
entertainer

MORGAN FREEMAN
actor

MARCUS GARVEY
black nationalist leader

JOSH GIBSON
baseball great

WHOOPI GOLDBERG
entertainer

CUBA GOODING JR.
actor

ALEX HALEY
author

PRINCE HALL
social reformer

JIMI HENDRIX
musician

MATTHEW HENSON
explorer

GREGORY HINES
performer

BILLIE HOLIDAY
singer

LENA HORNE
entertainer

WHITNEY HOUSTON
singer and actress

LANGSTON HUGHES
poet

JANET JACKSON
musician

JESSE JACKSON
civil-rights leader and politician

MICHAEL JACKSON
entertainer

SAMUEL L. JACKSON
actor

T. D. JAKES
religious leader

JACK JOHNSON
heavyweight champion

MAGIC JOHNSON
basketball great

SCOTT JOPLIN
composer

BARBARA JORDAN
politician

MICHAEL JORDAN
basketball great

CORETTA SCOTT KING
civil-rights leader

MARTIN LUTHER KING, JR.
civil-rights leader

LEWIS LATIMER
scientist

SPIKE LEE
filmmaker

CARL LEWIS
champion athlete

JOE LOUIS
heavyweight champion

RONALD MCNAIR
astronaut

MALCOLM X
militant black leader

BOB MARLEY
musician

THURGOOD MARSHALL
Supreme Court justice

TERRY MCMILLAN
author

TONI MORRISON
author

ELIJAH MUHAMMAD
religious leader

EDDIE MURPHY
entertainer

JESSE OWENS
champion athlete

SATCHEL PAIGE
baseball great

CHARLIE PARKER
musician

ROSA PARKS
civil-rights leader

COLIN POWELL
military leader

PAUL ROBESON
singer and actor

JACKIE ROBINSON
baseball great

CHRIS ROCK
comedian and actor

DIANA ROSS
entertainer

WILL SMITH
actor

WESLEY SNIPES
actor

CLARENCE THOMAS
Supreme Court justice

SOJOURNER TRUTH
antislavery activist

HARRIET TUBMAN
antislavery activist

NAT TURNER
slave revolt leader

TINA TURNER
entertainer

ALICE WALKER
author

MADAM C. J. WALKER
entrepreneur

BOOKER T. WASHINGTON
educator

DENZEL WASHINGTON
actor

J. C. WATTS
politician

VANESSA WILLIAMS
singer and actress

OPRAH WINFREY
entertainer

TIGER WOODS
golf star

RICHARD WRIGHT
author

ON ACHIEVEMENT

Coretta Scott King

Before you begin this book, I hope you will ask yourself what the word *excellence* means to you. I think it's a question we should all ask, and keep asking as we grow older and change. Because the truest answer to it should never change. When you think of excellence, perhaps you think of success at work; or of becoming wealthy; or meeting the right person, getting married, and having a good family life.

Those goals are worth striving for, but there is a better way to look at excellence. As Martin Luther King Jr. said in one of his last sermons, "I want you to be first in love. I want you to be first in moral excellence. I want you to be first in generosity. If you want to be important, wonderful. If you want to be great, wonderful. But recognize that he who is greatest among you shall be your servant."

My husband knew that the true meaning of achievement is service. When I met him, in 1952, he was already ordained as a Baptist minister and was working toward a doctoral degree at Boston University. I was studying at the New England Conservatory and dreamed of accomplishments in music. We married a year later, and after I graduated the following year we moved to Montgomery, Alabama. We didn't know it then, but our notions of achievement were about to undergo a dramatic change.

You may have read or heard about what happened next. What began with the boycott of a local bus line grew into a national crusade, and by the time he was assassinated in 1968 my husband had fashioned a black movement powerful enough to shatter forever the practice of racial segregation. What you may not have read about is where he learned to resist injustice without compromising his religious beliefs.

He adopted a strategy of nonviolence from a man of a different race, who lived in a different country and even practiced a different religion. The man was Mahatma Gandhi, the great leader of India, who devoted his life to serving humanity in the spirit of love and nonviolence. It was in these principles that Martin discovered his method for social reform. More than anything else, those two principles were the key to his achievements.

These books are about African Americans who served society through the excellence of their achievements. They form part of the rich history of black men and women in America—a history of stunning accomplishments in every field of human endeavor, from literature and art to science, industry, education, diplomacy, athletics, jurisprudence, even polar exploration.

Not all of the people in this history had the same ideals, but I think you will find that all of them had something in common. Like Martin Luther King Jr., they all decided to become "drum majors" and serve humanity. In that principle—whether it was expressed in books, inventions, or song—they found a goal and a guide outside themselves that showed them a way to serve others instead of living only for themselves.

Reading the stories of these courageous men and women not only helps us discover the principles that we will use to guide our own lives; it also teaches us about our black heritage and about America itself. It is crucial for us to know the heroes and heroines of our history and to realize that the price we paid in our struggle for equality in America was dear. But we must also understand that we have gotten as far as we have partly because America's democratic system and ideals made it possible.

We are still struggling with racism and prejudice. But the great men and women in this series are a tribute to the spirit of the country in which they have flourished. And that makes their stories special and worth knowing.

1

OSCAR GLORY

WHEN DENZEL WASHINGTON stepped on-stage at the Dorothy Chandler Pavilion in Los Angeles, California, in 1990 to accept the Oscar for Best Supporting Actor in a Feature Film, he joined the very short list of African Americans who have won this distinguished award. Although he had been nominated before, he had never won; the 35-year-old actor was now in the company of four other notable and gifted black actors: Hattie McDaniel, Sidney Poitier, Louis Gossett Jr., and Whoopi Goldberg.

Once the applause subsided, Denzel made his speech. The other nominees—Dan Akroyd, Martin Landau, Danny Aiello, and Marlon Brando—watched from the audience as Denzel graciously thanked his family and colleagues for their support.

The prestigious Oscar, the award most coveted by actors and actresses, is distributed annually in Los Angeles by the Academy of Motion Picture Arts and Sciences. The mission of the Academy is "to advance the arts and sciences of motion pictures and to foster cooperation among the creative leadership of the motion picture industry for cultural, educational, and technological progress." The Academy also aims to "recognize outstanding achievements by conferring annual Awards of Merit," otherwise known as the Oscars. The festive atmosphere surrounding an Academy Awards ceremony is surpassed only by the

Denzel Washington displays his Oscar for Best Supporting Actor for his role in Glory.

Sharts (Jihmi Kennedy), Trip (Denzel Washington), and Rawlins (Morgan Freeman) with other members of the 54th Regiment confront jeering white Union soldiers in the 1989 film Glory.

suspense of wondering whose name will be called when the sealed envelopes announcing award recipients are opened.

Every new movie that arrives in theaters is reviewed by the Academy—and by film critics and audiences—for its "Oscar-worthiness." The most well-known categories are Best Picture, Best Actor and Actress, Best Supporting Actor and Actress, and Best Director, but there are scores of other categories as well. In each category, five nominated people, films, or groups vie for the Oscar, a 13 1/2-inch, gold-plated statue that graces the homes of some of the most respected names in the industry. While the statue itself is of little monetary value, winning the award means more to most actors than a pot of gold. Denzel Washington was no different; as he stepped offstage, he proudly joined the elite group of actors and actresses with Oscars on their shelves.

By the time the 62nd Academy Awards ceremony was over, the film *Glory*, in which Washington had starred and for which he had received his award, had also won two Oscars, for Best Cinematography and Best Sound. And Washington's own reputation as an actor was now confirmed. He had already won the 1989 Golden Globe Award for Best Supporting Actor and was about to learn that he had received an NAACP Image Award in the same category. (The National Association for the Advancement of Colored People is an anti-discrimination organization founded in 1909.) His once-shaky film career was suddenly taking off.

Winning an Oscar was immensely satisfying for Denzel Washington. The actor had always stood by his convictions when choosing movie roles and had turned in a number of stellar performances. Ed Zwick, the director of *Glory*, was thrilled with Denzel's performance in the movie: "The camera is able to look deeply inside and see an inner process, if somebody has one. Denzel has an extraordinary inner life, and the camera is more than aware of it. I think you partake of that when he's trying to show so little to reveal so much."

The movie *Glory* is based on the true story of the 54th Regiment of the Massachusetts Voluntary Unit, the first black military unit to serve in the Civil War. In all, more than 180,000 black troops joined the Union army to support the abolition of slavery.

The 54th was headed by a young white officer named Robert Gould Shaw, played in the movie by Matthew Broderick. An inexperienced soldier, Shaw was eager to head his own regiment and consented to lead the 54th despite the fact that its existence was viewed by many whites as a joke. The 54th began as a disorganized and poorly trained group largely made up of uneducated former slaves. Among these men is

This memorial in Boston, Massachusetts, is dedicated to Colonel Robert Gould Shaw, commander of the all-black 54th Regiment commemorated in the film Glory. Shaw was played by Matthew Broderick.

"Trip" (Denzel Washington), an embittered ex-slave who ran away from his owner at the age of 12.

From the start of their training, the men of the 54th faced discrimination. They were denied guns, shoes, uniforms, and other necessary provisions given to all other Union troops. The black soldiers were not taken seriously in their attempts to serve in the war, and Shaw fought hard on behalf of his men for the respect he thought they deserved.

In the film, however, when Trip is caught leaving camp, Shaw feels it necessary to whip him in accordance with army regulations. The scene is disturbingly reminiscent of a slave owner flogging a runaway. What Shaw does not know is that Trip had merely gone in search of decent boots for his swollen, bloody feet.

But otherwise Shaw stands by his soldiers and they by him. When he receives word that any black Union soldier apprehended by a Confederate will be shot, he tells his men that they will receive an honorable discharge should they wish to avoid that possibility. All of the men stay. When the black soldiers discover that they are being paid less than white soldiers, the soldiers tear up their pay. In solidarity, Shaw follows suit by ripping up his own paysheet and convincing the other white officers, including his brother, to do the same.

When the unit finally makes it to the front line, they knowingly march into certain death to penetrate a Confederate-held area. In the ensuing battle they lose more than half of their company—including Trip and Colonel Shaw—but they have held their ground, both physically and metaphorically.

Although *Glory* itself received mixed reviews, Denzel Washington and the other actors who played members of the 54th Regiment, including Morgan Freeman, Jihmi Kennedy, and Andre Braugher, were praised for their performances. Washington told *California* magazine:

> I was happier making *Glory* than I've ever been working on a movie. We had a great deal of rehearsal time, which helped us lock in our characters, and I was playing a character that I really found interesting. He is somebody who makes people uncomfortable, because he's a racist. But he was made racist by racism. He lived the way he had to live, doing whatever it took to survive. He wasn't afraid, which I admire.

While Denzel admired the character of Trip, plenty of influential people were admiring him. The actor had carefully researched the role that African

Americans played in the Civil War. He improvised a great deal of his character's background, a fact especially evident in the scene where Trip talks about himself to the other soldiers while they are gathered around a campfire. "There were very few scripted lines," Washington told *New York* magazine. "I based my response on the personal history I had developed for my character—he was a runaway; he had lost his parents. I steeped myself in the reality I had formed for myself, so that when we got to that scene, it meant something more than just the words I was saying."

One of the most powerful scenes in the movie is the whipping scene. Washington does not speak as the camera focuses on his face. Tears flow as he thinks about his character and all that he has endured. "It just happened," Denzel said of the tears. "I was thinking that there is nothing else they can do to [Trip]." His expression is fierce rather than sad, however. "As the whipping commences," the *Village Voice* wrote, "Washington cuts [Matthew] Broderick one of those withering, contemptuous looks that brothers aim daily at racist or insensitive whites."

But *Glory* was not aimed solely at African-American viewers. One of the biggest draws of the film was its universal appeal. The theme of overcoming race and finding a common cause convinced Washington to appear in the film.

Prior to this performance, Washington had tackled several lead roles; his smaller part in *Glory* was considered by some to be a step in the wrong direction. But the quality of the script and the cast made it a smart move. Washington was noticed not only by the Academy of Motion Picture Arts and Sciences, the Golden Globes, and the NAACP, but also by many film critics—and by the moviegoing public. Washington was naturally pleased with his award-winning performance, but more importantly, he was pleased with the telling of the story. "I think the men of the Fifty-fourth would have liked the way we told their story," he said.

Through determination, hard work, and talent, Denzel Washington had finally arrived. But his path to success had not always been smooth.

2

THE PREACHER'S SON

DENZEL WASHINGTON WAS born on December 28, 1954, the second child of Denzel and Lennis Washington and the brother of sister Lorice. Denzel became the middle child after another son, David, was born.

Denzel grew up in Mount Vernon, New York, a largely middle-class suburb of New York City just north of the Bronx, where he was surrounded by children from varied ethnic and racial backgrounds. "[M]y friends were West Indians, blacks, Irish, Italians, so I learned a lot of different cultures," Washington recalls. He has affectionately called Mount Vernon "the safest and best community on the planet."

But in the 1950s, Mount Vernon's racial harmony was unusual. Most of America was not so lucky. Segregation was especially evident in the South, where it was legal to discriminate: drinking fountains were marked "Colored Only," buses and other public transportation had designated seating for blacks, and restaurants posted signs reading "Whites Only."

On December 1, 1955, however, a woman named Rosa Parks boarded a bus in Montgomery, Alabama, and, tired from her day as a seamstress in a busy department store, refused to give up her seat on the bus to a white man. She was arrested for breaking the law. The ensuing Montgomery Bus Boycott, led by civil-rights activist Martin Luther King Jr., would

Washington poses with a few of the many beneficiaries of the Boys and Girls Club of America. "We have a choice," Washington has said of the organization's work. "We can either invest in the lives of our children today, or pay for the tragedy of their failure in the future."

19

help end segregation and fuel the struggle for racial equality during the next decade.

In the film industry, life for African Americans was no different. Black actors of the 1950s and 1960s were defined by their race. Their roles were carefully circumscribed by discrimination—they played marginal characters, such as sidekicks, servants, or criminals. Denzel Washington remains fully aware of the difficulties faced by the generation of black actors before him. "Color is always important," he says. "It's important to me. I don't want to be colorless. I'm an African who lives in America. But in situations where it doesn't matter, it shouldn't." This conviction is evident in his career; many of the roles Washington chooses are decidedly nonspecific about race, yet he has also taken on roles in which his African-American heritage is essential to the character he plays.

Denzel's levelheadedness comes from his upbringing. The elder Denzel was a minister whose reverential spirit filled the Washington home. He also held other jobs so that his family could be financially secure, and during a time when most women did not work outside of the home, Lennis Washington also pitched in by running a beauty parlor. "She saw to it I was exposed to a lot of things," Denzel recalled of his mother. "She couldn't afford [life's finer things], but she was very intelligent. She is basically responsible for my success."

The younger Denzel learned from an early age to love God and value hard work as a means to success. At 12, he worked part-time at a local barbershop. He greatly enjoyed earning his own money: "Everybody looked like a dollar bill to me," he would later explain. Washington attributes his present success to this early willingness to work and claims that too many rising actors aren't willing to do so to achieve fame. "People have gotten away from the work," Denzel said with uncharacteristic vehemence in a 1994 interview with *Gentleman's Quarterly* magazine.

"[They] want to be at the right *party*, they want to get *rich*, they want to be *large*. . . . They want to be the one. They want it, and they don't know what's goin' on and how to get it. They don't!"

In addition to working at the barbershop, the young Denzel hung out at the Mount Vernon Boys Club, a safe haven from trouble. The good-looking youth played football and basketball, and before he reached high school he was already being noticed by girls. Dena Cook, a former cheerleader for the Mount Vernon Boys Club football team, told *People* magazine that around girls, Denzel "was always extremely shy. But what he didn't know was that he had lots of girls who liked him."

Washington has never forgotten his ties to the Boys Club (now called the Boys and Girls Club). He spent most of his time there; he recalls that "they practically had to kick me out at night." Today, he is the national spokesperson for the clubs. "For me it was Billy Thomas, my Boys and Girls Club director, who taught by example and challenged me to achieve my potential in life," Washington recently said in a press release for the organization's Union County, New Jersey, chapter. "I know that without his guidance and direction I would not be where I am today."

Denzel is featured in print advertisements for the clubs and is a firm believer in the organization's goal: helping the future of America by helping its children. "We have a choice," he said in the press release, "we can either invest in the lives of our children today, or

Escorted by her lawyer, Rosa Parks goes to jail on February 22, 1956, for charges of violating segregation laws in Montgomery, Alabama. Two months earlier, Parks had refused to give her bus seat to a white man. Her actions inspired Martin Luther King Jr. to arrange the Montgomery bus boycott, one of the earliest organized protests of the American civil-rights movement.

pay for the tragedy of their failure in the future."

It may have been the spirit of the club that helped Denzel through the tough times he faced in 1968, when he was 14. His sense of peace and security at home was suddenly shattered when his parents separated. Confused and upset, Denzel began running with a wild crowd and getting into fights at school. "You protect the part of yourself that's hurting the best way you know how, by fighting or closing yourself off—however you work it out," he said of his reaction to his parents' eventual divorce. His upbringing prevented him from getting into any serious trouble, but at his mother's insistence, he and his sister enrolled in boarding schools.

Denzel won a partial scholarship to Oakland Academy, a prestigious prep school for boys in upstate New York. The school's predominantly white student body was a stark change from the ethnic melting pot that Denzel had known in Mount Vernon. Although he was an average student academically, he excelled in extracurricular activities such as band and sports—especially football.

When Denzel became a senior and faced graduation, he still did not know what he wanted to do with his life. He did know, however, that he wanted to attend college. He applied to Yale and Boston Universities, but he was turned down by the former and would not have received enough scholarship money to attend the latter. Finally, he settled on Fordham University in the Bronx, not far from his childhood home. At Fordham, he began as a premed major in the fall of 1972 and later switched to journalism. After listening to his father's sermons for many years, Denzel had developed a gift for storytelling, but journalism proved to be the wrong medium. Frustrated by his failure, Denzel dropped out of school for a semester and temporarily entered the working world.

After unfulfilling jobs at a post office and a sanitation department, Denzel decided to return to college.

Determined to begin the new school year that fall, he found a seasonal job at a YMCA camp in Lakeville, Connecticut, that he had attended as a child. There, Denzel found a new avenue for self-expression.

As a child, Denzel had had limited exposure to film and theater. Reverend Washington made sure that his children were not exposed to what he considered the vulgarity of many Hollywood films. Denzel's early movie experiences were mostly Disney films and biblical epics, neither of which provided insight into the craft of acting or ignited in him a desire to perform.

At the Lakeville camp, Denzel was not only responsible for coaching sports, but he was also put in charge of assembling the camp talent shows. His experience onstage made him realize that he wanted to act. He seemed to have a natural talent for it and

One of Denzel Washington's first influences was professor and actor Robinson Stone, shown here (second from right) with costars in the 1953 film Stalag 17. Stone directed the Fordham University theater workshop that inspired Washington to pursue a career in acting.

Washington chats with Robinson Stone during the 1991 commencement exercises at Fordham University, where the actor was awarded an Honorary Doctor of Fine Arts.

only needed the proper direction and instruction to realize his full potential.

Denzel found that guidance when he returned to Fordham and enrolled in a summer theater workshop run by Robinson Stone, a literature professor who was also a professional actor (he had played "Joey" in the 1953 film *Stalag 17*). During one class, when Stone asked his students to describe their goals, Denzel claimed that he wanted to be "the greatest actor in the world."

While this statement might seem bold coming from someone so young and inexperienced, Denzel had faith in himself from the beginning. This confidence quickly caught on with those who saw him act. "A lot of actors need to prove something," said director Alan Pakula, who directed Denzel in the 1993 movie *The Pelican Brief*. "I don't feel that with Denzel. He doesn't have that torture, that self-doubt you find in some actors. Maybe it's a sense of self-belief."

This kind of composure may come easily after one has become famous, but to have it so early in life is remarkable. It would carry Denzel through many struggles as he pursued an acting career.

After his summer experiences with acting, Denzel decided to double major in drama and journalism. He saw journalism as an aid to a potential acting career. Washington has compared the process of researching his film characters to that of an investigative reporter following a story. For example, Washington read extensively and drew upon memories of his father speaking from the pulpit for his title role in *Malcolm X* (1992). The actor's intense exploration of his characters may explain why he is now considered one of today's most versatile actors.

At Fordham, Professor Stone admired Denzel's ability and cast him as the lead in the campus production of Eugene O'Neill's *The Emperor Jones* and as the title character in *Othello*. "I enjoyed learning the lines," recalls Denzel. "I enjoyed being out in front of people, I enjoyed the way they responded to me. Then someone said to me, 'You can do this for a living.'" Denzel was hooked.

Stone himself had once appeared in a production of *Othello* featuring the legendary African-American actor Paul Robeson. Nevertheless, Stone told the *Chicago Tribune*, "[Denzel] was easily the best Othello I had ever seen. . . . I remember [actor] Jose Ferrer came to look at it. He and I agreed that Denzel had a brilliant career ahead of him." In fact, Fordham faculty and alumni still talk about Denzel's amazing performance.

Stone convinced several film agents to see Denzel's performance. As a result, the young actor was offered his first professional role before he had even graduated from college. Denzel had landed what many struggling actors can only hope for—a part in a television movie.

3

STRUGGLING ACTOR

❦

IN 1977, AROUND the time Denzel graduated from Fordham, he made his debut as a professional actor in the television movie *Wilma*, which chronicled the life of African-American Olympic track star Wilma Rudolph. Washington played Rudolph's boyfriend.

But it was a young actress named Pauletta Pearson, in the role of runner Mae Faggs, who caught Washington's attention in real life. In an interview years after meeting Denzel, Pauletta told Oprah Winfrey, "I thought he was cute, but fell in love with his spirit. And then I thought, 'Hmmm, not a bad package.'"

Denzel was too nervous to give much thought to Pauletta: "It was my first day on my first film and all I remember feeling was fear. I had just graduated from college, I had never been in front of a camera before, and here I was this male lead in this TV film." Not long after, Denzel was accepted by the American Conservatory Theater (ACT) in San Francisco, California, one of the most prestigious training grounds for young actors.

Despite its reputation, however, ACT was not a good fit for the academically listless Washington. He decided that he would rather learn through experience than read and write papers about acting and the theater. One of Washington's former teachers, Joy Carlin, explains: "Some people who, like Denzel, are

Denzel Washington as a young actor.

"I liked his style," Pauletta Washington has said of her first meeting with her husband, while Denzel describes his wife as having been a "child prodigy." Here the two attend a benefit performance by Debbie Allen in Los Angeles in 1992.

naturals pick up the techniques quickly and incorporate them into their own technique. . . . I have the feeling he learned what he had to learn and then got a little bored."

Washington left ACT after one year, determined to test the waters of Hollywood. But his dream of making it big there did not materialize, and he eventually returned to New York—and to the often tedious life of a struggling actor.

There were, however, several factors that made the battle somewhat less difficult. One was the increasing number of roles available to black actors in theater. In the 25 years since the Montgomery bus boycott, the civil-rights movement had made great strides. With increased awareness came more job opportunities for blacks. In the acting world, a number of black-oriented theater groups were born, and Washington was fortunate—and talented—enough to get work with them. "It was an exciting time," he told *American Film* magazine:

> [My generation was] lucky. There were all these black theater folk. We came along at a good time, with different ammunition from the previous generation's. We came along—college educated. We were the first of the sixties and post-sixties era folk. It was the right combination.

For Denzel, another pleasant aspect of returning to New York was reuniting with Pauletta. They met again at a mutual friend's party and talked nonstop. Their encounter blossomed into a romance. The next night, by pure coincidence, they sat next to one another at a play in the city. Pauletta, whose friends were in the play, invited Denzel to the cast party downtown, and he suggested that they take a cab—a rare treat for two struggling young people. Pauletta remembers thinking, "I like his style." But Denzel didn't know just how far away the party was. "I was burning a hole in that [cab] meter with my eyes," he remembers, "I was like 'How many more blocks did you say the party is?'" When he finally admitted that he didn't have enough money to cover the fare, Pauletta contributed her week's grocery money. "But I still liked his style!" she later insisted.

After going east in 1978, Washington began landing acting jobs. Although he had told his his college professor that he wanted to be the greatest actor in the world, he had never particularly aspired to become a celebrity. In fact, Washington felt lucky just to be working steadily so early in his career. In the next few years, he appeared in Richard Wesley's *The Mighty Gents*, Sharon Pollack's *One Tiger to a Hill*, Ntozake Shange's *Spell #7*, Lonnie Elder III's *A*

Washington played actor George Segal's illegitimate son in his first feature film, the comedy Carbon Copy *(1981).*

Geechee Quick Magic Trance Manual and *Dark Old Men*, and Shakespeare's *Coriolanus*.

Although Washington was working regularly, his pay often did not cover his expenses, so he did not have his own apartment. Now 24, he lived at home in Mount Vernon with his mother and Pauletta, who had moved in that same year. Denzel commuted to Manhattan. The young couple knew that if they wanted to get married, they needed a more steady and reliable income.

Denzel saw an opportunity to remedy his financial situation when he was offered a feature role as a street hoodlum turned heavyweight boxer in the television movie *Flesh and Blood*, an adaptation of Pete Hamill's book of the same name. But though Washington did enjoy a higher salary for a while, the movie was not the "big break" he had initially believed it would be.

During the years that followed, Pauletta was the main breadwinner of the two. "My wife was a child prodigy," Denzel has proudly said of Pauletta:

> She was a Cliburn competitor at eight, nine years old. North Carolina School of the Arts, Juilliard [School of Music], masters in composition, the whole nine yards. She was a star at such a young age, she didn't have a childhood. When she did Broadway shows, she worked . . . with the best. When we met, she was making all the money.

And when it looked like Denzel might not become "the greatest actor in the world" because he was not getting any work, it was Pauletta who urged him to keep going. Washington did just that, and his persistence paid off. He eventually landed more prominent theater roles that placed him in the public eye.

The off-Broadway production of *When the Chickens Come Home to Roost* offered Washington what would be his first chance to play the black activist Malcolm X. The play's premise concerned a fictional meeting between Malcolm X and Elijah Muhammad, the head of the Nation of Islam. Although Washington had grown up during the 1960s when Malcolm X was most active, he knew little about the slain leader. "I didn't even have a view of Malcolm then," he revealed in a *New York Times* interview. "We just didn't listen to that kind of talk in my father's house." As always, the actor extensively researched his character. He read articles about Malcolm X, listened to taped speeches, and watched film footage of the man in an effort to create an authentic character.

The research paid off. Although the play was not financially successful and closed after only 12 performances, Denzel was praised by New York theater critics. According to Frank Rich of the *New York Times*, Washington was "firm, likable . . . honorable and altruistic without ever becoming a plastic saint." Washington was also honored for his performance with an Audelco Award. Even then, he had premonitions that he would play Malcolm X again. "When I did that play," he recalled, "I said to myself 'I know I'm going to do this movie one day. I know it.'"

Washington's first big-screen role came in 1981 in the movie *Carbon Copy*, in which he played the illegitimate black son of a white corporate executive (George Segal). Producer Stanley Shapiro knew that Washington was headed for stardom when he and Michael Schultz discovered Washington on the New York stage: "We spent three or four months looking for the right young man. We saw something like four or five hundred actors. They had to act and [also] be able to do comedy."

Immediately after *When the Chickens* closed, Washington began rehearsals for Charles Fuller's *A Soldier's Play*. Set on a fictional army base during World War II, the play explores the conflicts among black and white soldiers. Denzel played Private Melvin Peterson. The production was well received by critics and audiences and eventually won the

Washington (above, center, in glasses) as Private Melvin Peterson in Charles Fuller's award-winning production, A Soldier's Play. *The actor reprised his role three years later in the 1984 film version,* A Soldier's Story *(facing page).*

Outer Critics Circle award for Best Off-Broadway Play, the New York Drama Critics Award for Best American Play, and a Pulitzer Prize. Washington himself earned an Obie Award, and he was singled out by a number of critics for his "particularly impressive" performance. The *New York Times,* comparing this role to his earlier portrayal of Malcolm X, praised him for his characterization of "another, cooler kind of young renegade."

Denzel Washington believed that this was as good as it could get. "I didn't know what a movie star was," he told *Entertainment Weekly* of his early theater career. "You did a job. There was no point of reference—there weren't any black stars, really. . . . So there wasn't anybody to be like."

Washington was becoming an established name in theater. And though *Carbon Copy* had done poorly at the box office, television producer Bruce Paltrow (father of actress Gwyneth Paltrow) had taken notice of Washington. The young actor was about to get a very big break.

Paltrow tapped Washington for a role in his new TV hospital drama, *St. Elsewhere*. Denzel, however, was not convinced that this was the best move for him. "I wasn't crazy about doing a [television] series, because I thought you'd get too popular. But I was tired of breaking my behind for no money. I went to L.A. thinking, 'This is only going to be for thirteen weeks, anyway.'" As it turned out, the job lasted much longer than 13 weeks. Washington's role as Dr. Phillip Chandler was a breakthrough in TV's portrayal of African Americans. Chandler was a young doctor, a graduate of Yale University who worked with white colleagues. The show premiered in fall 1982 and ran for six years, garnering 12 Emmy Awards.

During the successful run of *St. Elsewhere*, Washington was able to fulfill many of his dreams, both

professionally and personally. As a secondary lead on the show, Washington had enough free time to pursue film and stage roles. He also wanted to propose to Pauletta, who had been with him for five years. But Pauletta was pursuing her own career in New York, and Denzel was often filming *St. Elsewhere* in Los Angeles, so he asked her to marry him during a telephone call. In 1983, the two were married—but they didn't have much of a honeymoon. Their schedules wouldn't allow it. "[S]he was doing *Jerry's Girls*, that went on to Broadway," Washington recalls. "After the wedding, on Sunday, I had to be back at Tuesday night's show [of *A Soldier's Play*]. The big honeymoon was at the Goodman Theater."

Professionally, Denzel was flourishing. The filming schedule of *St. Elsewhere* allowed him to take other roles during the show's breaks. When *A Soldier's Play*, which ran in Chicago and New York, was adapted for film, Denzel reprised his stage role as Private Peterson. The movie, entitled *A Soldier's Story*, arrived in theaters in 1984 to critical and popular acclaim. It eventually grossed $21.8 million.

In addition to his public roles of stage performer, television star, and movie actor, Denzel added the private role of father. In 1984, he and Pauletta had their first child, John David. The experience changed Denzel's life. He began to realize "the difference between life and making a living. I used to think what I did for a living was my life. Acting [was] my life," he said in an interview some time later. "When we had that first child, acting became making a living. The child was life. It's a miracle, an absolute miracle what happens."

Washington believes that becoming a father also affected his acting:

I think that fatherhood has loosened me up. I think I've always been funny. It has to do with the way I trained as an actor. I started off, I cut my teeth on *Oth-*

"This is only going to [run] for thirteen weeks," Washington thought when he began work on the set of the TV show St. Elsewhere, *which premiered in 1982. The show ultimately ran for six years and received 12 Emmy Awards.*

ello and Eugene O'Neill and Strindberg and *A Soldier's Play*, and that's what I became because that's what I did. When someone in your youth calls you a "serious actor," you say, "Yes, I am." As you get older, you learn how to simplify your life. I used to be more brooding, I think, than I am now.

Denzel wanted his child to have stability with his father, the stability that Denzel had lacked after his parents separated. Because his own father had disappeared from his life after the divorce, Denzel had been somewhat apprehensive about becoming a father himself. But he was also determined to be the best parent he could be. "I didn't have my father to teach me," he told *Essence* magazine in 1996. "That's why it's so important for me to be around for my son." Denzel and his father did not see one another for six years but finally reconnected when the younger Denzel was 20.

The same year that John David was born, Washington appeared as an assistant district attorney in another television movie, *License to Kill*, a story about the repercussions of a drunk-driving accident. His performance won him his most recent and most memorable television movie role as the title character in *The George McKenna Story*. The movie, based on a real-life inner-city school principal named George McKenna, showed how McKenna changed the lives of his students and transformed L.A.'s George Washington High from a school plagued by gang problems into a safe place to learn. In the movie, as in real life, McKenna succeeded in turning the school around, and George Washington students began winning academic awards.

Next on Denzel Washington's plate was a small movie role as a political lobbyist in Sidney Lumet's film *Power*. Washington's character, Arnold Billings, pulls the political strings that cause a U.S. senator who believes in implementing solar power to give up his senate seat. Billings hires Pete St. John (Richard Gere) to create a favorable public image for Democratic industrialist Jerome Cade (J. T. Walsh), in an effort to win Cade the vacant senatorial seat. The role marked Washington's first portrayal of a less-than-heroic character. Although not an outright villain, Billings's corrupt practices propel the story. Despite the lure of its big names, however, *Power* was a box-office disappointment.

Casting Denzel as a wealthy, behind-the-scenes man who controls the destinies of other (white) characters defied stereotypes of "appropriate" film roles for African Americans. "I think all films can speak to people across color lines," Washington remarked. "I don't think that's a new concept. Do you think that only Italians go see [Italian director Martin] Scorcese's films? That only Britons go see [British director Richard] Attenborough's films, that only Canadians go see Norman Jewison's films? You have to question that [line of thinking]. I think people go to *good* movies."

By 1986, 31-year-old Denzel Washington was a familiar face on TV and in Hollywood. But he had yet to get the break that would make him a celebrity. All that was about to change.

4

THE MAN WITH FIRE
IN HIS EYES

❧

"WE HAD TO have a man of charm, of erudition, of intellect, of perception, who was humorous, relaxed, yet confident," director Richard Attenborough said of his hunt for a black actor to play murdered South African political activist Steven Biko in the movie *Cry Freedom*. Attenborough auditioned more than 100 actors for the part before he saw *A Soldier's Story* and was convinced that Denzel Washington was his choice. But Washington wasn't so sure that he could take on such an assignment. The filming was in Zimbabwe, and he worried that his family and *St. Elsewhere* responsibilities would suffer should he accept the part.

The format of the film was also a problem for Washington. Although Steve Biko, a black man, is the subject of *Cry Freedom*, the plot unfolds through the eyes of Biko's biographer, a white newspaperman named Donald Woods. Attenborough believed that most moviegoers were not ready to accept a first-person narrative about a black revolutionary. But the positives outweighed these negatives, and after careful consideration Washington decided to take on the role.

In the movie, Donald Woods (Kevin Kline) writes an article in which he calls Biko a black racist. When an angry black doctor confronts Woods and says he should meet with Biko to hear the truth,

Washington as South African political activist Steven Biko in the 1987 film Cry Freedom. *Denzel described his first trip to Africa for the movie's filming as being "like a homecoming."*

Denzel Washington and actor Kevin Kline on the set of Cry Freedom.

Woods agrees—out of amusement more than any sincere attempt to discover the truth. Eventually Woods befriends Biko and learns the hardships of being an outcast firsthand when he becomes the object of the same police harassment that Biko has experienced. When Biko dies mysteriously in a jail cell, Woods dedicates his life to uncovering the truth about his friend's death.

To prepare for the role, Washington not only read about the real Steven Biko and learned to imitate a South African accent, but he also deliberately gained 30 pounds so that he would look more like the solidly built activist. In addition, he cultivated a goatee and removed the caps from his front teeth.

Traveling to Africa, which Denzel originally considered one of the drawbacks of accepting the role, turned out to be one of the best aspects of making the movie. Although it was his first visit there, he described his arrival as feeling "like a homecoming." Moreover, meeting South Africans while filming opened his eyes to the devastating effects of apartheid (official racial segregation). Washington later spoke about the experience:

> I went over there with all my American anger and energy. I thought, What's wrong with all those crazy white South Africans? I'm going to get all the brothers together, and we're going to go get them! That was Western ignorance. A lot of those people have been fighting for twenty years. They've lost fathers and sons and brothers and sisters. All they want is peace. I just felt a little small after meeting them.

The experience helped Washington to understand the enormous obstacles facing Steven Biko, which in turn made his portrayal of the activist more powerful. (Washington was so impressed by the land of his ancestors that he returned in 1996 with his wife for their 13th wedding anniversary. The couple renewed their vows in an early-morning ceremony officiated by a different kind of activist, Archbishop Desmond Tutu.)

For the first time since receiving an Obie Award for *A Soldier's Play*, Denzel was recognized and lauded by critics as an outstanding actor. "I bring myself to any part," Denzel has said of his acting technique. "And I'll bring my experiences and voice my opinions." He imbued the character of Steven Biko with realism and humanity, presenting a noble and glorious portrait of the activist. Despite Washington's original concern that the movie told the story of Biko through the eyes of a white man, it was Denzel who captured the critics' eyes and viewers' hearts. *New Yorker* magazine declared that "every time Biko, in his mustache, goatee, and long sideburns, returns and we hear his pungent, rolling cadences our interest quickens; this man with fire in his eyes commands the screen— Denzel Washington is the star by right of talent."

Although *Cry Freedom* was only mildly successful at the box office, Denzel Washington was remembered at Oscar time, receiving a nomination for Best Supporting Actor. While the award ultimately went to Sean Connery for his performance in Brian De Palma's acclaimed film *The Untouchables*, the fact that Denzel was included among the top actors in Hollywood signified that he had become a force in the industry. He was now being offered plum roles in motion pictures.

Surprisingly, however, Washington's next project was in the theater, where he had also enjoyed critical success. This time, Denzel was making his first appearance on Broadway starring in Ron Milner's *Checkmates*. Performing in such a production is a dream of many actors: Broadway contains the most respected and best known theaters in New York City. The name itself has come to symbolize the pinnacle of success to theater actors.

Starring on Broadway would be difficult. Washington was still playing Phillip Chandler on *St. Elsewhere*, which filmed 3,000 miles away in Los Angeles; and like most Broadway shows, *Checkmate*'s performance schedule was grueling. In addition, Pauletta was pregnant with their second child, a daughter whom they would call Katia.

But Denzel had the opportunity to work with Ruby Dee and Paul Winfield, two very talented African-American actors. Determined to be a success in his role as Detroit liquor distributor Sylvester Williams, Denzel researched his character more thoroughly than usual. He worked briefly for a liquor distributor to find out what made Williams tick. Unlike the venerable Steven Biko in *Cry Freedom*, Williams is a common man with flaws that often outweigh his good qualities.

With a Broadway credit and the success of his Steven Biko role under his belt, Denzel looked forward to landing a starring role in another film. He found the right vehicle for his talent in the British film *For Queen and Country*. Washington played

Denzel Washington hugs his onstage wife, Marsha Jackson, in a scene from Ron Milner's Checkmates. *The production marked Washington's first appearance on Broadway.*

Ruben, a British soldier home from fighting in the Falkland Islands, where Great Britain had defeated Argentina. Once back in England, Ruben learns that the country he believed in and risked his life to protect is racist and corrupt. He is, however, essentially powerless to change it; he must learn to come to terms with his status as a black man in a powerful, white-run government.

As Ruben, Denzel lit up the screen. Unfortunately, the film was never released in the United States because its distribution company went bankrupt. Washington would have to wait a while longer for critical and financial success.

Denzel's personal life was already successful and happy, however. By this time he and Pauletta had been married for five years and had two beautiful, healthy children. The TV series *St. Elsewhere*, which

Trip (Washington) and other soldiers of the 54th Regiment storm a heavily fortified Confederate fort in Glory. Washington described his character as "somebody who makes people uncomfortable. . . . He lived the way he had to live, doing whatever it took to survive."

had given Denzel valuable exposure and provided a jumping-off point for other ventures, wrapped up its final season in 1988. Having left television work behind, Washington now turned his complete attention to establishing a film career.

His next role, as Xavier Quinn in the movie *The Mighty Quinn*, gave him a chance to tackle another leading role—this time as an enforcer of the law. Quinn is a police chief on a nearly crime-free Caribbean island. He lives a peaceful life until the evidence in the death of an affluent white man points to the policeman's best friend. Quinn must uncover the facts of the murder to clear his friend and solve the crime.

Although critics praised Washington's performance, *The Mighty Quinn* was a box-office disappointment, grossing only $4 million. But it had presented a solid view of a healthy black relationship—something rarely seen in feature films. Washington and his onscreen wife, played by Sheryl Lee Ralph, enjoy a romance far different from previous depictions of black relationships. Ralph described her joy at seeing "a black couple that's healthy, together, and trying to work it out. Nobody's kicking anybody's butt, nobody's hooking or pimping or whatever. We're a wholesome couple having some problems that we're trying to work out."

In part because of this role, black and white audiences alike had begun to notice Denzel Washington. In the late 1980s heyday of "'hood" movies, Washington chose to play middle-class African-American men struggling to make better lives for themselves and their families, rather than portraying angry and often stereotypical blacks taking revenge on the world around them. Washington has avoided the latter type of role because he does not want to be pigeonholed as a "black actor." While he enjoys watching such movies, he feels that this genre may be exhausted. "I grew up with murder and mayhem, too, but I'm trying to turn it into [a] positive," he has said. Because of his desire to represent "the average guy," Washington is one of the few black actors routinely given roles originally intended for white actors. For this reason, he doesn't feel that he has missed out on anything. Of fellow superstars Kevin Costner and Tom Cruise he says, "They haven't made any movies that I wanted to make."

Washington's next role would be as a far different character in an entirely different world—a black Civil War infantryman in the movie *Glory*. His moving performance as Trip earned him an Academy Award for Best Supporting Actor and catapulted him into the rarefied world of the most sought-after screen actors.

As the newest leading black man, it then seemed

natural for Washington to team up with the leading black director in Hollywood, Spike Lee. Lee wanted Washington for the part of Bleek Gillam in his new film *Mo' Better Blues*. But while Denzel was known primarily as a mainstream actor who played roles in which his race did not necessarily define the character, Spike Lee was famous for his controversial depictions of black culture and of black neighborhoods and their inhabitants.

Mo' Better Blues, loosely based on the life of the great jazz trumpeter Miles Davis, tells the story of Bleek Gillam, a self-absorbed womanizer—characteristics very different from those Denzel had incorporated into his previous on-screen personas. Starring opposite Denzel were the rising black star Wesley Snipes and Spike Lee himself.

As always, Washington carefully studied his character, and he learned how to play the trumpet so that his close-ups would seem more realistic. He met Miles Davis and watched him perform. It was the first time that Washington had worked with an African-American cast and crew and with Spike Lee. He was very happy for the chance to work with his "contemporaries," he said. "Spike and I worked very closely, and I did more improvisation in [*Mo' Better Blues*] than I ever have."

Mo' Better Blues did not launch Washington into superstardom. But it did establish him as one of Hollywood's best-looking film stars. Spike Lee recalled going to the theater to see the film and hearing women in the audience scream, "Not the face!" during a scene in which Bleek is beaten. Denzel's good looks landed him on *People* magazine's "50 Most Beautiful People List" nearly every year in the 1990s; in 1996 the magazine dubbed him the "Sexiest Man Alive."

Despite his new status as a sex symbol, Denzel Washington admits that love scenes make him uneasy and that he prefers not to do them, which may help explain why his characters usually are not

Always a thorough researcher, Washington learned how to play the trumpet for his role as jazz musician Bleek Gillam in Spike Lee's 1990 film Mo' Better Blues.

portrayed in that light. On the days that he was scheduled to shoot love scenes in *Mo' Better Blues*, Washington felt tense and irritable. At one point the actor even refused to take off his shirt. "He'd say, 'I'm a family man. I don't want to do that,'" Spike Lee told *USA Today*. "Like most of us, Denzel is not an exhibitionist," a friend told *People* magazine. "I think he's just being the preacher's son."

Around this time the preacher's son decided to take another break from films, this time to perform the title role in the New York Shakespeare Festival's production of *Richard III*. The performance was one of the few for which Washington received harsh critical reviews. One reviewer called him "surprisingly . . . muted." Another questioned his credentials for playing a Shakespearean character. Although Washington is "an actor of noteworthy achievement," *New York* critic John Simon said, "This Richard speaks [in] something perilously close to a monotone." But with movie scripts stacking up and offers rolling in, Denzel was soon lured back to Hollywood and moviemaking.

"The appeal of *Heart Condition*," Denzel said of his second 1990 movie, "was to do something lighter than I'd been doing to stretch a little. Also, I'd been on the road for two years, in Africa, Jamaica, London, and Georgia. This offered a chance to shoot at home and to have some fun. I hope the movie will open up a lot more opportunities for me." Denzel played the suave lawyer Napoleon Stone opposite British actor Bob Hoskins as Jack Mooney, a bigoted Los Angeles cop who miraculously receives Stone's heart in a transplant after Stone is murdered by a senator's henchman to cover up the politician's illegal activities. The racist Mooney not only ends up with the heart of a black man, but he is also compelled to help Stone's ghost find his killer.

Unfortunately, *Heart Condition* was panned by critics and avoided by audiences. Denzel himself had won praise for tackling a comedy role, albeit one with a less-than-sparkling script. After *Heart Condition*, however, the actor decided to try another genre— this time he would be an action hero.

In the 1991 movie *Ricochet*, Washington is a rookie cop named Nick Styles who becomes a hero when he brings down a notorious bad guy (played by John Lithgow).

One thing Denzel enjoyed about playing an action hero was the feeling of being in great physical shape. "I haven't had a thirty-inch waist since I was eighteen," he exclaimed during the filming. "But I'll be happy when the film is over and I can go back to eating ice cream."

But the actor ultimately was disenchanted by the violence and mayhem of the action film. Three years later he told *Gentleman's Quarterly* magazine, "*Ricochet* was the last time I sat in a movie and went 'I can't—this is not me. I can't do this kind of movie. 'Cause this is mindless violence. I can't be a part of this.'" Denzel's tentativeness must have come through on the screen because both audiences and critics disliked the film.

In the end, however, Denzel saw his action-hero experience as another experiment in broadening his skills: "I shouldn't say *Ricochet* was a mistake," he said. "It's not one of my favorite films. But I talk to people, and some go, 'Man, that was one of the best movies you ever made.' So who am I to say?"

Perhaps because of this experience, Washington made sure that his next film, *Mississippi Masala*, not only showcased his talent but also started with an outstanding script. Although the production company was on a very limited budget and could not afford to pay Denzel his usual asking price, he was willing to make an exception for such a high-quality movie.

In the movie Denzel plays Demetrius Williams, a man living in the small town of Greenwood, Mississippi, who meets an Indian woman named Mina. Because of the narrow-minded views of the towns-people and the expectations placed upon them by their families, Mina and Demetrius have to hide their love. When it is revealed, they must choose between tradition and each other.

Mississippi Masala premiered to rave reviews. It was Washington's first love story, and his acting was not only believable but also commendable. *People* magazine declared that his performance would "make a believer out of anyone who ever doubted that he is an A-list movie star and sex symbol." But Washington received an honor even greater than mere critical praise: the NAACP awarded him another Best Actor Award for his portrayal of Demetrius Williams.

Denzel Washington was on a high both in his career and at home. Pauletta had just given birth to their third and fourth children—twins, Malcolm and Olivia. The proud father could not have been happier—and his best film work still awaited him.

Washington in his starring role in the 1990 New York Shakespeare Festival production of Richard III.

5

"THE BEST THAT IS IN HIM"

IN 1975, AFRICAN-AMERICAN author James Baldwin wrote in his book *The Devil Finds Work*: "Not one [black American actor] has ever been seriously challenged to deliver the best that is in him." Sixteen years later, Denzel Washington would try to change that assertion, taking on the most challenging, rewarding, and critically acclaimed role of his career—truly the best that was in him. Interestingly, it would be a role that he had already played on the stage.

Years before, when he had performed in the off-Broadway production *When the Chickens Come Home to Roost*, Denzel believed that he would play Malcolm X again. He was right—when he was offered the lead in the film adaptation of the life of Malcolm X, Washington jumped at the opportunity. He was more than excited about his second chance to play the black militant leader. "This is a story about the evolution of a man," he maintained. "It's a spiritual, philosophical, political evolution. My prayer is to illustrate that and have that be some kind of *healing* for people."

Even before filming began, the movie, titled *Malcolm X*, was steeped in controversy. The original director of the movie was Norman Jewison, who had also directed *A Soldier's Story*. But filmmaker Spike Lee told Warner Bros., the studio producing the film, that he was determined to take on the project. "I

"People saw him as a racist leader and in some ways he was," Denzel Washington said of the title character in Spike Lee's 1992 film, Malcolm X. "But you have to see behind the scenes to try and figure out why."

Washington's uncanny likeness to slain activist Malcolm X (above) astonished many people, especially those who had known the militant black leader during his lifetime.

have a big problem with Norman Jewison directing The Autobiography of *Malcolm X*," Lee said. "That disturbs me deeply. It's wrong with a capital 'W.' Blacks have to control . . . films [about black leaders]. Malcolm X is one of our most treasured heroes. To let a non-African American do it is a travesty." Lee's remarks set off a debate within the studio and in Hollywood over whether it is appropriate to have a white director for a film about a black activist—or whether it mattered at all.

Eventually, Jewison bowed out of the project and Lee took over. He overhauled the preproduction work that had already been done, keeping only Denzel Washington from the original cast. Having

worked with the actor in his film *Mo' Better Blues*, Lee knew the scope of Washington's talent. He also rewrote the screenplay, basing it not on Malcolm X's 1965 autobiography but on a 1969 book written by James Baldwin and Arnold Perl.

Washington was determined to turn in an unforgettable performance. Although he had studied for this character before, he wanted to learn still more about him for the extensive film, to find out why he did and said the things that made him both popular and feared. "People saw him as a racist leader and in some ways he was," admitted Washington. "But you have to see behind the scenes to try and figure out *why*."

Malcolm X was the most prominent and vocal

Director Spike Lee sports a cap emblazoned with a large X. The fashion swept the country after the successful release of Malcolm X. "Half the people [wearing the X] did not even know what they were promoting," Washington said later.

leader of the Nation of Islam, a religion based on the teachings of an itinerant salesman named Wallace Fard, who in the 1930s began preaching a mix of Christianity, Islam, and black nationalism to the poor blacks of Detroit, Michigan. According to the Black Muslims (as Nation of Islam members are known), blacks were the "original men," rulers of the world. In order to recover their sovereignty, they must separate themselves completely from whites. The Nation of Islam has strict moral and disciplinary codes, and daily prayer is vital. Devout followers eat only one meal a day and follow dietary restrictions similar to those of traditional Muslims.

In addition to studying the Black Muslims, Washington tried to follow these religious and dietary codes to get a feel for the way a Black Muslim lives each day. Since Malcolm X had a lankier frame than Washington, the single-meal rule also helped the actor stay slender so that he would more closely resemble the activist.

Malcolm X is a lengthy and serious film tracing the brief life of a great leader who overcame a tragic childhood and a prison sentence to become one of the most influential African Americans in U.S. history. Malcolm X was born Malcolm Little in 1925 in Omaha, Nebraska. The family moved to Michigan when Malcolm was four and was plagued by attacks from the Ku Klux Klan, which had resurfaced during the 1920s. It is believed that Klan members murdered Malcolm's father, Baptist preacher Earl Little, who openly spoke out against racism. After struggling to support eight children on her own, Malcolm's mother, Louise, eventually had an emotional breakdown and lost custody of them.

By age 10, Malcolm was in a detention center. Five years later, he moved to Boston to live with his half-sister, Ella. But he was attracted by the city's glamour and soon became enmeshed in drug-dealing and theft. By the time Malcolm Little was 20, he was serving a 10-year prison sentence for robbery.

Several years into his sentence, the angry, antisocial Malcolm began to have a change of heart. Inspired by an intelligent and articulate elder inmate (named Baines in the film) and by letters from his brother and sisters describing their newfound religion called the Nation of Islam, Malcolm set his sights on improving and educating himself.

He learned the teachings of Elijah Muhammad, the leader of the Black Muslims, and began to develop a sense of pride that he had never before experienced. While still in prison, he converted to the Nation of Islam, dropping his surname "Little" because it symbolized his ancestors' enslavement and adopting an X as his last name.

Upon his early release from prison in 1952, Malcolm moved to Detroit and joined other members of the growing Nation of Islam. Exuberant over being a free man and at having found himself within the Nation, Malcolm eagerly set about recruiting new followers. Elijah Muhammad was especially impressed with his eloquent and aggressive new disciple, and Malcolm quickly rose within the Nation's ranks. Nine years after converting, Malcolm was appointed the national minister of the Nation of Islam, second in power only to Elijah Muhammad. Malcolm X's energetic—and highly controversial—message that the "white man is the devil" and that blacks are destined to rule the earth attracted the attention of both blacks and whites.

Eventually, however, Malcolm X began to see hypocrisy among his fellow Black Muslim leaders, many of whom envied his power and favored status. Elijah Muhammad, who had always preached against sexual promiscuity and adultery, was accused of fathering four children with two of his former secretaries. Malcolm was deeply distressed by the news and confronted the leader, who did not deny the truth of the accusations. On the other hand, convinced by

Shortly before his death in 1965, Malcolm X made a spiritual pilgrimage to Mecca, which drastically changed his views on racism and religion. Here Washington portrays Malcolm X praying in a Muslim mosque.

other ministers that Malcolm sought to displace him, Elijah Muhammad began taking steps to reduce his national minister's power. The rift between the two became permanent later that year when Muhammad suspended Malcolm from his duties.

Ultimately, Malcolm broke away from the Nation to form his own organization, called Muslim Mosque Incorporated. But by then he had received numerous death threats, which he believed to have been issued by the Nation of Islam. On February 21, 1965, during a speaking engagement in Harlem's crowded Audubon Ballroom, Malcolm X was assassinated in front of his wife and four daughters. He was 39 years old.

Working on this emotionally charged story drained Denzel Washington, but he also faced a sad period in his personal life. During the filming of *Malcolm X*, the elder Denzel Washington, then 81, died. Although the younger Denzel's father had been absent from his life for some time after the divorce, their relationship had been improving in recent years, and the actor was drawing on memories of his father's preaching to portray the charismatic speaker Malcolm X. He was devastated by the loss.

Although Reverend Washington had admired the peace-preaching Martin Luther King Jr. rather than the militant Malcolm X, Denzel was profoundly saddened that his father would never see him in this role. His sister, Lorice, said after seeing the film: "[Denzel's] hand gestures and the rhythms of his voice were Daddy's."

Other difficulties followed. Even after Spike Lee assumed responsibility for *Malcolm X*, budget problems arose that Warner Bros. refused to address. In an effort to avoid shelving the film, Lee appealed to a number of prominent African Americans for financial support. The Artist Formerly Known as Prince, Oprah Winfrey, Bill Cosby, Magic Johnson, and many others eventually contributed more than $5 million; Lee himself raised another $6.5 million by selling the foreign rights to the film and donating two-thirds of his $3-million salary to make up the difference between the movie's cost and what the studio was willing to pay. "I don't care what the budget is," Lee firmly stated. "I don't care what the contract says. Nothing's going to hurt the movie."

On November 20, 1992, *Malcolm X* opened to packed movie theaters. It was a milestone in the film world—the first epic motion picture ever made about a black figure. Despite its length—more than three hours—it grossed $2.4 million on its opening day alone.

Malcolm X was arguably the biggest film of 1992. Not only did the film awaken many Americans to the complex and difficult character of Malcolm X, but it also, surprisingly, fueled a fashion rage. "Malcolm-mania" had arrived. Before the film's release, Lee and the studio had heavily marketed it by printing hats and T-shirts emblazoned with large Xs. But the fashion may have gone too far. It bothered Denzel Washington that some of the people sporting the X did not even know what they were promoting. "Half the people walking around don't even know that the X has anything to do with our film," he said. "I mean, ain't no X hats in our picture."

But for those who did know what the X meant, the film was a triumph. For the first time, Washington had starred in a black film whose story was told from a black perspective. "Everything I have done as an actor has been in preparation for this," he said proudly.

In the long run, however, the movie received mixed reviews, although Washington himself, who called it the "most controversial film of the decade," received high praise for his performance. To many audience members—and to some of those who had known the real Malcolm—Denzel Washington nearly *was* Malcolm X. "It was very eerie watching Denzel," said A. Peter Bailey, a professor at Virginia Commonwealth University who had worked with Malcolm to establish the Organization of Afro-American Unity (OAAU) during the last year of Malcolm's life. "He captured the nuances and mannerisms of Malcolm so well. [Malcolm] was not a violent man. He had a tender side to him." And though Spike Lee himself was just a boy when Malcolm X was slain, he too was amazed by Denzel's performance: "It was scary, being on that set, it was spooky," he said. "It was not Denzel, [it] was Malcolm."

Denzel not only bore a striking resemblance to

the slain activist, but he also brought to life Malcolm's power as a speaker and a leader, especially for those born after Malcolm's death. Not long after the movie's release, awards and nominations flooded in for Washington. He received the New York Film Critics Circle Award for Best Actor, the Boston Film Critics Association Award for Best Actor, the Chicago Film Critics Award for Best Actor, the Berlin Film Festival Silver Bear Award for Best Actor, and the MTV Movie Award for Best Male Performance; he was also nominated for Best Actor by the Golden Globe and Academy Award committees.

But while the awards were fine tributes, Washington knew that doing the best he could was all that mattered. "I didn't lose any sleep before or after [the Academy Awards ceremony]," he told *Gentleman's Quarterly*. "It sounds like the stock answer, but it's true. . . . I want to be the best actor in the world. I was taught that's what you're supposed to try to be—the best."

Denzel Washington was now one of Hollywood's hottest stars. Yet his primary goal—becoming the best actor he could be—had not changed. He had known that he wanted to reach that goal since his first day of drama class at Fordham University. After seeing his striking performance in *Malcolm X*, many people were convinced that he had achieved it. But Denzel was not about to stop reaching for perfection.

6

MAKING MUFFINS

✿

Denzel Washington once described a film as "just like a muffin. You make it. You put it on the table. One person might say, 'Oh, I don't like it.' One might say it's the best muffin ever made. One might say it's an awful muffin. It's hard for me to say. It's for me to make the muffin."

Following the success of *Malcolm X*, Denzel would make a lot of "muffins," most of which would be hits. But he now faced a problem shared by many actors when they finish a role in which they truly shine: can there possibly be a better role in store? Some actors become so well-known for playing one particular part that they have difficulty topping themselves. While the role of Malcolm X had been incredibly challenging and rewarding, Denzel was determined to keep working toward excellence. And after the intense work of playing a murdered activist, Denzel wanted to play a lighter, more relaxed part, a role with more laughs and less screen time.

Although offers to do blockbusters were pouring in, Washington decided instead to accept a role in British actor-director Kenneth Branagh's unique adaptation of Shakespeare's play *Much Ado About Nothing*. Washington's character, Prince Don Pedro, was part of a magnificent ensemble cast that included Emma Thompson, Robert Sean Leonard, Keanu Reeves, and Michael Keaton.

Washington accepts an award from the city of Los Angeles for his charitable work as his wife, Pauletta, and their children, Olivia, Katia, Malcolm, and John David, look on.

The film was scheduled to be shot in the Italian countryside. Washington decided to take the part "because of Kenneth, because it's Shakespeare, and because it's something that will test me as an actor. Kenneth is doing something unique: making Shakespeare accessible to everyone," he said. The actor also viewed the film as a refreshing change of pace from the usual mainstream movies. "[It's] kind of art house, fun for me. One for [myself]," he told *Entertainment Weekly*. Although critics had frowned upon Denzel's undertaking a Shakespearean character in the stage production of *Richard III*, he had grown as an actor and felt confident in his ability and in the new project.

The part was originally intended for a white actor. But Denzel's acting talent transcended color. Whereas Malcolm X's color defined his role in society, Prince Don Pedro was a far different character, one who could be played by any talented actor. Denzel had gone from playing a part that could be realistically played only by a black man to one in which racial identity had little bearing. He had found his follow-up role.

Much Ado About Nothing is a comedy of wild antics, absurd misunderstandings, and a happy ending. In the film, Prince Don Pedro acts as the liaison between two young lovers, Claudio (Robert Sean Leonard) and Hero (Kate Beckinsale), fueling the romance and arranging a marriage. The plans progress nicely until the intervention of Don Pedro's illegitimate brother, Don John (Keanu Reeves). Don John hates Claudio and plots to break up Claudio and Hero's union by staging a pretend tryst between Borachio, one of his own followers, and Hero's maid, Margaret, who is disguised as Hero. The wedding eventually occurs, however, and a blossoming romance between the two comic leads, Hero's cousin Beatrice (Emma Thompson) and Benedick (Branagh), hints of another wedding in the near future.

The cast of the 1993 film version of Shakespeare's Much Ado About Nothing, *left to right: Michael Keaton, Robert Sean Leonard, Keanu Reeves, Kate Beckinsale, Emma Thompson, Kenneth Branagh, and Denzel Washington.*

The film was mildly successful at the box office, grossing $22.5 million; Washington himself received mixed reviews. A few questioned the idea of a black man playing what was considered a white role, but most critics were more open-minded. Branagh, Denzel's director, had nothing but praise both for the actor and his abilities: "[Denzel Washington] has intellectual weight, spiritual gravity, and a powerful . . . romantic presence."

Washington's next project was a film adaptation of John Grisham's best-selling novel *The Pelican Brief*. Grisham's fast-paced legal thrillers—and the screenplay versions of them—were proving timely, wildly popular, and hugely successful. For Washington, it also made "good business sense" to accept a role in a film starring the popular actress Julia Roberts, who had earned fame for her roles in films such as *Steel Magnolias* (1989) and *Pretty Woman* (1990).

In *The Pelican Brief*, *Washington Herald* reporter Gray Grantham (Washington) gets involved with Darby Shaw (Roberts), a Tulane University law student whose life becomes endangered after she writes a legal paper, or brief, about the possible motive behind the murders of two Supreme Court justices. Shaw's report, called "the pelican brief" because it implicates an oil company that is endangering the habitat of the Louisiana brown pelican, causes an immediate scandal in the political circles of Washington, D.C.

Gray Grantham is a serious character, and Washington plays him carefully opposite Roberts's Darby Shaw. He let Roberts shine while playing his part with vitality. *The Pelican Brief* was the first movie in which Washington appeared that broke the $100-million mark. And the critical reaction was as enthusiastic as that of the moviegoers. *Entertainment Weekly* raved about Washington, "[I]t's doubtful whether there's a smarter leading man working today. . . . the actor shuts the doors of his face and

gets us wondering how he'll react."

Denzel also received praise from other cast members and from director Alan Pakula. During a scene with fellow actor John Lithgow, Pakula told Denzel: "You remind me exactly of Robert Redford—you have that look," referring to Redford's reputation as the "thinking woman's heartthrob." But Denzel did not need—or want—to be known for his looks alone. Rather, he wanted his acting skill to speak for itself.

Julia Roberts, meanwhile, expressed disappointment that her character and Washington's did not share an on-screen kiss. She told Oprah Winfrey that working with an actor of Denzel's fame was like "working with the Beatles. I'd come out of my trailer, and there'd be four guys going, you know, 'Hey Julia, babe.' . . . Denzel comes out . . . and [there were] 200 women just screaming." When asked why

Actress Julia Roberts hand-picked the down-to-earth Washington to star opposite her in the 1993 adaptation of John Grisham's novel The Pelican Brief. *Of her costar, Roberts said, "Denzel is very grounded in who he is and what he's doing and why he's doing it."*

she had handpicked Denzel to be her costar even though his character was supposed to be white, she said simply, "I wanted the best man for the role."

Thanks to his smart role choices, fine performances, and natural good looks, Denzel had become one of the "A-list" stars in the business, and his asking price soared to more than $8 million per film. His popularity also allowed him the freedom to fashion his own work schedule and spend more time with his family.

In addition to spending time with their own children, Denzel and Pauletta also generously donate their time and money to charities and organizations that benefit other children, such as the Boys and Girls Clubs of America. They have contributed $1 million to the Nelson Mandela Children's Fund and participate in a citywide Christmas toy drive each year.

The Washingtons also support the Gathering Place, a Los Angeles AIDS clinic. The couple has bought a van and raised more than $250,000 for the clinic. Dorothy Brown, director of the women's and children's programs, was touched by the lack of fanfare that accompanied Denzel's first arrival at the clinic. "The guy came in here by himself," she told *Gentleman's Quarterly*:

> No entourage. Sat on the floor with the women and babies. We need volunteers to play with babies while the women meet. He sat with a baby for *three hours on the floor*. And he listened to the women. Some of them, that mattered more than their AZT [medication for AIDS patients]. . . . See, someone who mattered told them *they* mattered. He gave them years. He gave them a reason for living.

Denzel and Pauletta's work at the Gathering Place had acquainted Denzel with AIDS firsthand. His experiences would help him to perform his next role more realistically—a homophobic lawyer who defends a gay AIDS patient in a lawsuit against his former employers. The movie, called *Philadelphia*, was directed by Jonathan Demme, the Academy Award-winning director of *Silence of the Lambs*. *Philadelphia* had attracted a top-notch cast, including Tom Hanks as the young lawyer afflicted with the disease.

Once again, the character played by Washington was originally written for a white actor. But to Demme, race did not matter in this role. He told GQ magazine that he had "always wanted to work with this amazing actor":

> Then I'm doing this white-bread [movie called] *Philadelphia*. The next thing I know, I'm on the phone to Denzel Washington. But this part is not African-American. I said, "You've read the script—do you think we have to make any adjustments in a character who is in theory written as a European person?" Denzel said, "No. Do you?" I said, "No, I don't." Then I got excited. It never wore off.

The film was controversial because it tackled two difficult issues—homosexuality and the AIDS virus—that had never been directly addressed on the big screen before. AIDS was initially believed to be a "gay disease" because it was first detected in homosexual men. The fear of becoming infected with a fatal disease became linked in many people's minds with the prejudices already held against homosexuals. But when the virus that causes AIDS began spreading among heterosexuals, it became clear that the disease has less to do with sexual orientation than with sexual activity. In other words, it is not a gay disease but a sexually transmitted disease that is spread through infected blood and other bodily fluids.

Denzel Washington's character, Joe Miller, is a lawyer, an average family man, and a homophobe (one who fears or discriminates against homosexuals). A self-proclaimed "ambulance chaser," Miller earns most of his pay by appearing at the scene of accidents or tragedies and convincing those involved

*Tom Hanks as Andrew Beck-
ett and Denzel Washington as
Joe Miller in the highly
acclaimed film Philadelphia.
Washington said that playing a
homophobic lawyer who agrees
to represent a gay man dying
of AIDS allowed him to learn
more about himself and his
own prejudices.*

to hire him as their lawyer.

One day, another lawyer named Andrew Beckett
(Tom Hanks) appears in Miller's office looking pale
and ill. Beckett has been unfairly let go by his former
employer, one of the largest law firms in Philadelphia, Pennsylvania, because he has AIDS. He is
unable to find anyone to represent him and has finally resorted to seeking help from Miller. Miller acts
the way an uninformed person might upon learning
that someone with AIDS is nearby: he is afraid to
touch Beckett, afraid he might "catch" AIDS or
transmit the HIV virus to his wife or infant daughter.
Miller declines to take Beckett's case, and Beckett

has no choice but to represent himself in court. Only when Miller later meets Beckett in a public library, surrounded by law journals—and by the stares and whispers of people who are aware of his condition—does Miller decide to help the man.

As always, Washington thoroughly researched his character by interviewing personal injury lawyers and watching courtroom cases so that he could play an attorney convincingly. For the other aspect of Joe Miller—his bigotry—Denzel found that he had to dig deep to find a part of himself that could summon such feelings. His character's prejudice against gays is a central part of the film. But the depth of Miller's prejudice surprises even himself: he has never faced his fears about homosexuality and AIDS. As Miller gets to know Beckett and Beckett's family and friends, he slowly discards his prejudice, having discovered that his view of homosexuals is unrealistic. Far from being a one-dimensional stereotype, Andrew Beckett is a passionate, intelligent, and loving man—who is also gay and dying of AIDS.

Washington, who had played the object of prejudice and had experienced it in real life, was now playing someone who inflicted his prejudices upon others. "I had to say to myself, 'Does it feel good to say that? How do you *really* feel?'" In the process of learning about Joe Miller, Denzel learned more about himself and his own prejudices:

> I didn't think I was [prejudiced] at all. I said, in general [before researching the role], "I have no problems with homosexuals, and I want to do everything I can to end AIDS." . . . I think that, much like the character—I don't think I am anything like the character, first of all—but I think I got a chance to vent certain frustrations, maybe. It was a good education.

While Denzel was studying his character, Tom Hanks was also working hard to understand Andrew

Beckett. The two actors sometimes joked around on the set to alleviate the heaviness of the movie's story line. The physical and emotional demands of Hanks's role were exhausting. Because Beckett's health declines drastically during the course of the film, Hanks wanted to drop weight as filming progressed so that he could realistically portray the "wasting" that a dying AIDS patient experiences. To tease his costar, Washington would fill Miller's briefcase with Milky Way candy bars and open it off-camera while Hanks was being filmed in the courtroom scenes. Despite the temptation, Hanks kept his weight down—and won the 1993 Oscar for Best Actor.

Denzel could not have been happier for his colleague: "I saw his dedication—how focused and disciplined he was," he said of Hanks. Although Washington himself received no awards for his performance, he earned stellar reviews. *The Los Angeles Times* declared that Washington had outdone his own performance in *Malcolm X*: "It was once thought an almost scientific impossibility that Washington could top his performance as . . . Malcolm X, but [in *Philadelphia*] he seems to redefine intensity and passion." The *New Republic* called it "his best performance since *Glory*." And the movie itself was a huge hit, earning more than $80 million in its first month. Its controversial subject matter seemed to spark a nationwide discussion about homosexuality and AIDS. One reviewer also praised director Jonathan Demme for using a black actor—Washington—to "embody the mainline audience's uneasiness over the gay lifestyle."

Tom Hanks took a professional risk in playing a gay character in a movie about AIDS. But Washington was also singled out for his courage in playing a homophobe. In an article for the *New Republic*, Andrew Sullivan said that the film "brazenly took a black, straight movie icon and made him grapple with a gay man. Denzel Washington's role for this reason took far more social bravery than Hanks's." Denzel himself was pleased with the movie and with his own performance, saying, "This is one of the first films I've been in where I didn't see something I wish wasn't in there."

Washington also received praise from his fellow actors in *Philadelphia*. Lisa Summerour, who played Joe Miller's wife, told *People* magazine in 1994, "I was expecting to feel nervous or starstruck. But he has a way of making you feel comfortable. He doesn't need attention or accolades. It was very refreshing." Hanks was also impressed with Washington: "I don't think Denzel is into the power or flash," Hanks told *Entertainment Weekly* in 1996. "I think he's into it because he has a great amount of dedication to what it is to be an actor."

Philadelphia and *The Pelican Brief* were released within a week of one another, during the Christmas season of 1993. Thus Denzel Washington had the good fortune of appearing in two very different, very well-advertised mainstream films at a time of year when many Americans have the time and the inclination to go to the movies. This timing only added to the huge success of both films. "I don't know if it was because of *Philadelphia* or *The Pelican Brief* or both, but I can see the difference in my career as a result of these two films," Washington noted. "There's a lot of people who would never go see *Malcolm X* or *Cry Freedom* or *A Soldier's Story*, but they'll go see Julia Roberts and Tom Hanks. And they'll see me and say 'Well, he's good too.' Then all of a sudden, you're there."

Washington finally had what he had been working for—commercial success in films that were not dubbed "black" movies, as *Glory* and *Malcolm X* had been. Not only had he fulfilled his personal desire for excellence, but he had also become an undeniable superstar.

7

GOD AND MUNDY LANE

❦

ALTHOUGH DENZEL WASHINGTON had been less than pleased with *Ricochet* and had vowed never to do another action picture, the year 1995 found him reversing his decision. His son John David was a big reason for the change of heart. "He was like, 'Dad, my friends are talking bad about me because you keep doing these old-folks movies. You've got to do some action movies,'" Washington laughs. "I said, 'All right. All right.'"

The movie *Crimson Tide* hooked him because of its other star, Gene Hackman. The story, which Washington described as "a good balance between substance and action," deals with the conflict between two naval officers, Captain Frank Ramsey (Hackman) and Lieutenant Commander Ron Hunter (Washington) aboard a nuclear submarine. On the brink of war with Russia, Ramsey and Hunter wait for orders to fire a nuclear warhead. When the order comes, the sub dives just as another message is coming through. The second message is cut off, and Ramsey insists that they should fire the missile. Hunter believes, however, that they must know the second order before taking action.

Washington as Easy Rawlins in Devil in a Blue Dress, *1995.*

What follows is a nail-biting, edge-of-your-seat thriller that was hailed as a great success. Of Hackman and Washington, *Entertainment Weekly* raved, "the two actors turn the film into a riveting Oedipal

Lieutenant Commander Ron Hunter (Washington) confronts submarine commander Captain Frank Ramsey (Gene Hackman) in the 1995 action film Crimson Tide.

duel. . . . What holds us is the sight of two superlatively fierce actors working at the top of their game."

Denzel was definitely at the top of his game. Although he had a starring role and top billing, he also showed his ability to work closely with his costar, Hackman. *Crimson Tide* was one of the box-office hits of 1995, grossing almost $92 million. Denzel had fulfilled his promise to John David to star in an "action" film. But he wasn't finished. Around the same time that *Crimson Tide* opened, another vehicle of Washington's, called *Virtuosity*, was released. The second film, however, was a flop. Washington later realized that he should have believed in his initial reluctance to take the part.

Set in 1999, *Virtuosity* was meant to be a science fiction thriller focusing on Parker Barnes, a former member of the Los Angeles Police Department who is imprisoned after he exacts revenge on the murderer of his wife and daughter. When the Law Enforcement Technology Advancement Center (LETAC) unleashes its virtual-reality android named Sid 6.7, Barnes is released in order to capture the havoc-wreaking cybervillain.

Denzel called *Virtuosity* "one of the hardest films I've ever done." Calling the experience an "education," he said that he had "never been in a film where there was so much computer-generated technology." Although he had made his son happy, he vowed once again to avoid doing action films. "I don't like them," he remarked. "You gotta run and jump and you don't talk. It's not acting."

After the success of *Crimson Tide*—and the misstep of *Virtuosity*—Washington was determined to return to serious acting. He was also set to launch a new enterprise, in which he would also be playing a role behind the cameras. In 1990, Washington had formed his own production company called Mundy Lane, which developed projects for Tri-Star Pictures. The company name came from the street where Denzel had grown up, where he had learned about race and accepting people of all ethnic backgrounds, and where he had played with his friends and dealt with his parents' divorce. Working with screenwriter and director Carl Franklin and executive producer Jonathan Demme, Washington prepared not only to act in his next project but also to coproduce Mundy Lane's first feature film.

The movie, *Devil in a Blue Dress*, was based on the 1990 novel by Walter Mosley. It tells the story of black private eye Easy Rawlins who, unemployed and on the verge of losing his home, takes on a detective job and gets involved in investigating a murder. Easy has to find a woman named Daphne, the girlfriend of mayoral candidate Todd Carter. Although she appears to be white, Daphne is known for associating with African Americans. Easy searches an illegal club that he frequents and questions his acquaintances. After spending the night at his friend Coretta's house, he gets a lead from her. But in the morning, after Easy leaves, Coretta is murdered. Easy is the main suspect in this murder, and he now needs to solve two mysteries—that of the missing Daphne and of the murdered Coretta.

Easy's search leads him to another body and photographs of the mayor in compromising situations. When he solves the mysteries and clears his name with the police, Easy becomes a wealthy man. But he has gone through the wringer for his money.

There are definite issues of race in *Devil in a Blue Dress*. Set in the postwar era of the late 1940s, the film tackles the issue of police brutality against African Americans (Easy is beaten when he is arrested for the murder of Coretta), the concept of "mixed blood" (Daphne cannot marry Todd Carter because she is half black), and the relatively new concept of a single, black man owning a home in a safe, suburban neighborhood.

The film, which cost $20 million to produce, received good reviews but was not popular with moviegoers; it earned only $16 million. While Washington was disappointed that more people did not see his movie, he tried to keep it in perspective. "They say period pieces are hard [sells]," he remarked. "We also opened the weekend of the O. J. Simpson verdict, you know, which didn't help. . . . [But] making fifty million dollars the first weekend is not the criterion for whether it's a good film."

Devil in a Blue Dress highlighted yet another multifaceted character in Washington's expanding repertoire. "Washington is sure, sharp, and sexy in what may turn out to be his signature role," *People* magazine enthused. The actor seemed to fit his part so well that many people thought Mosley had written it with Denzel in mind. In truth, Washington had always been at the top of the list to play Easy Rawlins, but he

had had impressive competition from actors such as Danny Glover, Wesley Snipes, and Tim Reid, all of whom had been considered for the part.

After a break from filming, during which Washington and his family traveled to Africa on a safari, the actor returned to Hollywood ready to begin a new project. His next movie, *Courage Under Fire*, was a big-budget project from 20th Century Fox costarring Meg Ryan. Harrison Ford and Tom Hanks had both been considered for the male lead, investigating attorney Lieutenant Colonel Nathaniel Serling. But Washington won the role in the end with a contract for $10 million—the highest salary Hollywood had ever paid to an African-American actor in a dramatic role. "After one action guy, two killers, three

For his performance in Courage Under Fire *(1996), Denzel Washington, shown here with Lou Diamond Phillips, earned the highest salary ever paid to an African American in a dramatic role.*

escaped cons, whatever, I said, 'This is interesting,'" Denzel told *Entertainment Weekly* of his first reading of the *Courage Under Fire* script. "It was different. It was, if you will, literature."

Colonel Serling is not only fallible but also unlikable at times. A man with a penchant for drinking, Serling becomes distressed as he learns about the circumstances surrounding the death of pilot Karen Walden, the first female candidate for a Medal of Honor. As Serling hears conflicting accounts of her behavior before her death, he reflects on his own past mistakes. Viewers learn that Serling had inadvertently killed one of his own comrades during the Gulf War. He went along with an official military cover-up of the tragedy and even lied to the man's relatives by telling them that the soldier had been killed by enemy fire. The stress of recalling these events leads Serling to drink heavily—but also makes him determined to get to the truth of what happened with Karen Walden.

Washington initially thought that his character was a little thin, so he decided to fill in the gaps with thorough research. In a 1996 interview with *Entertainment Weekly* he described his preparations:

> I sat down with the DA [district attorney], psychiatrists, and alcoholics. I went to the [U.S. military] National Training Center up at Fort Irwin and fired their M1A1 tanks and I fired the .50 calibers. I went out on battle simulations that they do with choppers and planes and tanks and 2,000 soldiers, and lived out in the field and sat with colonels and watched them almost break down talking about the loss of soldiers.

More than ever, Denzel felt that research was crucial to playing his role well: "The research I did made me understand the importance of integrity," he said in another interview. "When you ask men and women to put their lives on the line for you, you have to prove that you're worthy for them to say, 'Yes, I'll go.'

It's a tough job. There's no middle ground in war."

Courage Under Fire did well at the box office, even though it opened in 1996 against summer blockbusters such as *Independence Day* and *Phenomenon*. It also received standout reviews. Denzel's inspired performance spurred rumors of an Academy Award nomination, but the honor never materialized. Once again, Washington was unfazed. "My concern," he said, "is raising the standard of work, not complaining about someone not voting for me."

8

"A LITTLE HUNGER IS GOOD FOR YOU"

I N *THE PREACHER'S WIFE*, a remake of the 1947 film *The Bishop's Wife*, Denzel Washington plays an angel sent to earth to help the title character (played by Whitney Houston) and her minister husband (Courtney B. Vance) build a church. Once again, Washington had great stakes in the movie's success: he was the producer as well as the star. Mundy Lane developed the project.

The movie was released by Walt Disney Pictures during the 1996 Christmas season. Unlike Washington's previous movies, it is a family film. But the actor had no problem changing genres. He told the Internet magazine *Mr. Showbiz*:

> To be involved in a film that is kind of feel-good, Christmassy, sweet, syrupy, if you will—some may even say corny—I don't think there's anything wrong with that. I've done films with the edge, drama, weight, and all that. I just thought we had an excellent opportunity to talk about faith and family.

The film also granted Washington the unique opportunity to sing with pop superstar Whitney Houston. Although Pauletta is an accomplished singer, Denzel knew that his own vocal skills were lacking, especially when compared to someone like Houston. "I'd given in to the fact that I was going to sound bad, so I said, 'Let me sound especially bad.' I

As family members look on, Denzel imprints his hands in the cement outside Hollywood's Mann's Chinese Theater. Washington was named to the "walk of fame" in 1998.

Washington—the son of a preacher—portrayed an angel on an earthly mission to help a minister and his wife (played by Whitney Houston) in The Preacher's Wife.

was a bit nervous. . . . That was a stretch for me," he said after the filming.

Playing an angel, however, presented a problem that Denzel had never before faced in his career: how would he research the part? He decided that one way would be to study the Bible. As time passed, he realized that this exercise was also helping him to see himself in a better light. "You get up in the morning and see how, not how angelic you are, but how helpful you are, how kind you are. . . . What I really found is that I like me better. I felt better."

The Preacher's Wife premiered against one of the biggest movies of 1996, *Jerry Maguire*, starring Tom Cruise. But Washington, too, was a selling point for audiences, and the film was a great success. It was also a first for Hollywood: never before had so much money—over $60 million—gone into an all-black movie. The fuss over this "first" was lost on Denzel's costar Whitney Houston, however. "What's so alien about us?" she asked during the movie's promotion. "I don't understand why there's such a big thing about all-black casts. I've seen movies with all-white casts. . . . It's a movie. Either you like it or you don't." And audiences did like *The Preacher's Wife*.

In January 1997, Washington received the prestigious ShoWest Actor of the Year Award for his outstanding achievements in *Courage Under Fire* and *The Preacher's Wife*. ShoWest, the largest annual convention in the world devoted exclusively to the motion picture industry, draws delegates from five continents. "I am especially honored to receive this award," Denzel said upon accepting it, "because it represents the feeling of those people who know film and support it—the theater-owners who show my movies and the audiences who go see them."

For all his fame and the awards he has earned, Washington has never allowed such acclaim to go to his head: "I try to be ego-less, if there is such a thing. I try to stay humble and hungry . . . just hungry to be good at my job. A little hunger is good for you." His success has allowed him to pursue passions other than acting: a few years ago, the Washingtons and a dozen of their friends opened a southern-style restaurant called Georgia on trendy Melrose Avenue in Los Angeles. Closer to home, Washington coaches his 13-year-old son John David's football team and his 10-year-old daughter Katia's basketball team.

Aside from God and his family, however, acting is Washington's first love and one that he plans to continue indefinitely. He also feels that he has worked too long and too hard to give it up. Audiences flock to his films, and the monetary rewards have increased with each movie—he received $12 million for his role in the 1998 dark thriller *Fallen*, in which he plays Hobbes, a Chicago detective who discovers that the culprit in a series of murders is an evil spirit. Also opening in 1998 was *He Got Game*, an intense drama directed by Washington's friend Spike Lee, in which Washington plays a temporarily freed prisoner.

Of course, as one of the hottest actors in Hollywood, Washington is always surrounded by talk of future projects. Spike Lee, rumored to have bought the rights to a biography of baseball great Jackie Robinson, has made it known that Denzel is his first choice to portray the player who broke baseball's color barrier. And Denzel fans may get the chance to see him don a top hat and tails as Duke Ellington in Irwin Winkler's adaptation of *Lush Life: A Biography of Billy Strayhorn*. (Will Smith, fresh from his megahits *Independence Day* and *Men in Black*, is interested in the part of Billy Strayhorn.)

In 1998, Washington was also listed as number 10 on the Harris Poll's "Most Popular Movie Star" survey, with actors such as Clint Eastwood, John Wayne, and Mel Gibson. No other black actor, male or female, was among the top 40 names.

With all of the wealth and success Washington has achieved, he still allows himself few indulgences. Were it not for his collection of expensive cars and his family's spacious home in Beverly Hills, California, one might not guess that Denzel is a film star. In addition to helping out at the Gathering Place and acting as national spokesperson for the Boys and Girls Clubs of America, Washington and Pauletta have pledged $2.5 million to their church, the West Angeles Church of God in Christ.

But such generosity is not surprising to those who know the actor well. When asked to prioritize his

Washington as Hobbes in the 1998 thriller Fallen.

life, Denzel has stated simply, "God, family, work, football." It is a rare Hollywood star who will proclaim, as Washington has, "God is my hero." And when *Essence* magazine asked in 1996 what he tells his children about the privileged life they are leading, Denzel replied:

> I try to explain to them that all they see around us, the things we have, are not of my doing. I am not the reason we have these things. God is. I want them to realize that you don't have to stab anybody in the back. You don't have to scratch anybody's eyes out. Just be honest, work hard and have faith. That will take them further in life than anything.

The award-winning actor becomes an audience member as he mingles with the crowd gathered to see Spike Lee's film Girl 6 in March 1996.

Denzel is not concerned with being a role model for blacks, yet he has become one. His willingness to work hard and his ability to transcend race throughout his career are inspiring to people of all ages and colors. He believes that excessive anger over the injustices one endures is a waste of energy. "Racism is a given," Denzel said while filming *Malcolm X*. "The question becomes: How do you deal with it? Get *busy* with yourself." He knows, too, that success and fame do not inoculate one against racism. He has been denied a cab and subtly snubbed in elevators or other closed-off places by women who, consciously or unconsciously, hold their purses more tightly in his presence. But he views such situations with humor and pragmatism. "I want to take out my wallet and say, 'Honey, don't worry about it. I think I've got a couple of more dollars than you.'"

After years of dedication to his craft, Washington is still aware of who he is. "I don't know if I have what a Stallone or a Schwarzenegger has to turn out blockbusters. I'm not that kind of action-hero type," he says. "I could be a [Tom] Cruise, maybe. I'm not complaining."

Then he adds, "None of these guys I've mentioned has an Academy Award, and I know all of them want one." He recalls fondly, "I looked out at all those big stars the night I won [my Oscar] and thought about that. I thought you can't have it all. . . . But you can try. And you know I will!"

CHRONOLOGY

1954	Denzel Washington born on December 28 in Mount Vernon, New York

1954   Denzel Washington born on December 28 in Mount Vernon, New York

1969   Parents divorce; enters Oakland Academy in upstate New York

1972   Graduates from Oakland Academy; enrolls at Fordham University

1973   Drops out of Fordham temporarily; returns and declares a dual major in drama and journalism

1977   Wins first professional acting role in TV movie *Wilma*; meets Pauletta Pearson; graduates from Fordham; moves to San Francisco to study at the American Conservatory Theater (ACT)

1978   Drops out of ACT and returns to New York; works in theater productions

1979   Stars in TV movie *Flesh and Blood*

1981   Wins Audelco Award for stage portrayal of Malcolm X in *When the Chickens Come Home to Roost*; wins Obie Award for performance in *A Soldier's Play*; stars in his first feature film, *Carbon Copy*

1982   Plays Dr. Phillip Chandler on TV series *St. Elsewhere* (the show runs for six seasons)

1983   Marries Pauletta; son John David is born

1984   Stars in TV movie *License to Kill* and feature film *A Soldier's Story*

1986   Plays title role in TV movie *The George McKenna Story* and appears in feature film *Power*; daughter Katia is born

1987   Nominated for Academy Award for Best Supporting Actor in *Cry Freedom*

1989   Feature films *For Queen and Country*, *The Mighty Quinn*, and *Glory* are released

1990   Wins Academy and Golden Globe Awards for Best Supporting Actor in *Glory*; stars in *Heart Condition* and Spike Lee's *Mo' Better Blues*; forms Mundy Lane production company

1991   *Ricochet* opens; twins, Malcolm and Olivia, are born; father, Denzel, dies

1992   *Mississippi Masala* and *Malcolm X* premiere; nominated for Best Actor Academy Award and Golden Globe Award; wins Chicago, Boston, and New York Critics Awards for Best Actor; receives Berlin Film Festival Silver Bear Award for Best Actor; wins MTV Movie Award for Best Actor

1993	Appears in Shakespeare's *Much Ado About Nothing*; stars in *The Pelican Brief* and *Philadelphia*
1995	Stars in and coproduces *Devil in a Blue Dress*; *Virtuosity* and *Crimson Tide* are released; wins NAACP Best Actor Award for *Crimson Tide*
1996	*Courage Under Fire* and *The Preacher's Wife* open
1997	Wins ShoWest's Actor of the Year Award for 1996
1998	Stars in *Fallen*, *He Got Game* and *The Siege*; listed as one of the Harris Poll's top 10 most popular movie stars; named to the Walk of Fame at Hollywood's Mann's Chinese Theater
1999	Named to the Harris Poll's top 10 most popular movie stars list; stars in *The Bone Collector* and *The Hurricane*
2000	Wins Golden Globe Award for Best Actor in a Drama for *The Hurricane*; nominated for a Screen Actors Guild Award and Academy Award for Best Actor for *The Hurricane*; stars in *Remember the Titans*

FURTHER READING

Brode, Douglas. *Denzel Washington: His Films and Career*. Secaucus, New Jersey: Birch Lane Press, 1997.

Farley, Christopher J. "Pride of Place." *Time*, 2 October 1995.

Hardy, James Earl. *Spike Lee*. Philadelphia: Chelsea House Publishers, 1996.

Lambert, Pam. "Heat from a Cool Source." *People*, 29 July 1996.

Masters, Kim. "Testing the Faith." *Time*, 16 December 1996.

Nickson, Chris. *Denzel Washington*. New York: St. Martin's Press, 1996.

Richmond, Peter. "Invisible Man: Is Denzel Washington More Than the Sum of His Parts?" *Gentleman's Quarterly*, January 1994.

Robotham, Rosemarie. "A Love Story: Denzel and Pauletta." *Essence*, December 1996.

Rummel, Jack. *Malcolm X*. Philadelphia: Chelsea House Publishers, 1989.

Simels, Steve. "Denzel Takes the A-Train." *TV Guide*, 22 August 1997.

FILMOGRAPHY

Wilma (TV movie, 1977)

Flesh and Blood (TV movie, 1979)

A Soldier's Play (stage, 1981)

Carbon Copy (1981)

St. Elsewhere (TV series, 1982–1988)

License to Kill (TV movie, 1984)

A Soldier's Story (1984)

The George McKenna Story
    (TV movie, 1986)

Power (1986)

Cry Freedom (British, 1987)

For Queen and Country (British, 1988)

The Mighty Quinn (1989)

Glory (1989)

Mo' Better Blues (1990)

Heart Condition (1990)

Ricochet (1991)

Mississippi Masala (1992)

Malcolm X (1992)

Much Ado About Nothing (1993)

The Pelican Brief (1993)

Philadelphia (1993)

Devil in a Blue Dress (1995)

Virtuosity (1995)

Crimson Tide (1995)

Courage Under Fire (1996)

The Preacher's Wife (1996)

Fallen (1998)

He Got Game (1998)

The Siege (1998)

The Bone Collector (1999)

The Hurricane (1999)

Remember the Titans (2000)

Training Day (2001)

John Q (2001)

INDEX

PICTURE CREDITS

page

2: Photofest
3: Archive Photos
10: Reuters/Corbis-
Bettmann
12: Photofest
14: Corbis-Bettmann
18: Courtesy Boys & Girls
Club of America
21: UPI/Corbis-Bettmann
23: Archive Photos
24: AP/Wide World Photos
26: Archive Photos
28: AP/Wide World Photos
30: Photofest

32: Photofest
33: Photofest
35: Photofest
38: Photofest
40: Photofest
43: Photofest
44: Photofest
47: Photofest
49: Photo © George E.
Joseph
50: Photofest
52: UPI/Corbis-Bettmann
53: Photofest
54: AP/Wide World Photos

56: Photofest
60: Photo Fitzroy Barrett/
Globe Photos
63: Photofest
65: Photofest
68: Photofest
72: Photofest
74: Photofest
77: Photofest
80: Photo Fitzroy Barrett/
Globe Photos
82: Photofest
85: Photofest
86: AP/Wide World Photos

ANNE E. HILL holds a B.A. in English from Franklin and Marshall College, where she wrote for *Franklin and Marshall Magazine*. This is her first book for Chelsea House. She lives in Wayne, PA, with her husband, George.

NATHAN IRVIN HUGGINS, one of America's leading scholars in the field of black studies, helped select the titles for the BLACK AMERICANS OF ACHIEVEMENT series, for which he also served as senior consulting editor. He was the W. E. B. DuBois Professor of History and Afro-American Studies at Harvard University and the director of the W. E. B. DuBois Institute for Afro-American Research at Harvard. He received his doctorate from Harvard in 1962 and returned there as professor in 1980 after teaching at Columbia University, the University of Massachusetts, Lake Forest College, and the California State University, Long Beach. He was the author of four books and dozens of articles, including *Black Odyssey: The Afro-American Ordeal in Slavery*, *The Harlem Renaissance*, and *Slave and Citizen: The Life of Frederick Douglass*, and was associated with the Children's Television Workshop, National Public Radio, the Boston Athenaeum, the Museum of Afro-American History, the Howard Thurman Educational Trust, and Upward Bound. Professor Huggins died in 1989, at the age of 62, in Cambridge, Massachusetts.

Denzel Washington /
J Washington HIL   **31057001197592**

Hill, Anne E.,
WEST GA REGIONAL LIBRARY SYS